The Poetic works of a Black man

The heart and soul of a man

Henry Epps

This book is dedicated to the women in my life, Vera and my

daughters Chimere, Chanise, Charise, Chatise and Kim. Much Love!

Table of Contents

I

Emasculation of the Black man

"The emasculation of the black man has been instituted from day one!

We hate, fear and despise each other and still we are the "Native Son"

We look alike, and we think alike, but we do not love the image of me,

In our streets we sell drugs, fear, violence even our souls for a fee,

They say we are free but are we free in deed?

We enjoyed the 70's "*Blackexplosion*" of movies about pimps and players,

And today we see our communities dying with so much need,

Now we are ball players, shot callers and player haters,

We prance around on the television like minstrel clowns.

Making fun of black men and putting each other down.

Yes, some have left the cause for a dollar or two,

And they care less for me or you!

Today they serve the mighty dollar and exploit our people

It makes you want to holler!

How long emasculated man will, you stand,

With your hand, open wide to serve that fake man?

Preachers preaching about money and exploiting our people,

With fake sermons and fake steeples,

They have ship wrecked the faith to chase that mighty dollar,

They parade around the pulpits, slick and cool

And, Peddling lies and mistruths as if we are fools!

How long emasculated black man will, you be shaken?

How long black man will your voice be taken?

It is a new day and together black man we must stand together,

We must learn to love our selves even a society that says whatever!

Yes black man I got your back, but not in the" *down-low whack!"*

We are destroying our communities from within,

And if we do that how can we ever win?

So this is the dilemma you see,

I need you and you need me,

Remember the words of Rodney King,

"Why we just can't get along" is my thing!

So the conclusion of the matter is this,

Support the black man because no one else will,

Go back and get a brother, let that be your wish,

And together if we believe one day, we will be strong,

Because the emasculation of my brother I say, it is wrong!

~Original work by Henry Harrison Epps Jr

II

Awaken my Bother

Awaken my brother to the truth of today,

We are being destroyed in every way,

We are killing each other for a penny or a dime,

And we must stop the madness before we run out of time!

Awaken brother and stop the madness,

Stop the killing and destruction of our black communities,

Raise your son to be a man,

And not be statistic in this barren land,

Awaken my brothers with power and fame

And reach back to your brothers

Who are calling your name?

And help the struggling mothers,

Awaken my brother's kings of hip-hop,

Your little brothers are listening to the messages send

And want to be like you on top,

Be careful little brother before you leave in an early end,

Original work by Henry Harrison Epps Jr

III

My Mother's Son

Hey momma why can't you love me,

Like I love you?

Why don't you understand?

That I have to stand and live like a man,

Hey, momma I know you are mad at dad,

And I know he made you made,

But can't you see he is not me,

That I am and always will be your little baby?

Hey, momma I have to face life troubles and strife

I have to choose the path for my life,

And I must live or die with decisions

Even thou they may bring life collisions!

Hey, momma do not let me go,
Yes, I am leaving but I have to let you know,
That you are my first love of my life,
And you have taught me how to select a wife!

Because when I see you, I see the best in love.
And you have taught me worship the God above,
Thank you momma for all you have done for me
And you have taught me how to be strong and free,

I know men have let you down in past,
And it is that fear of men that you try to mast,
But remember momma I just want to make you proud of me.
And thank you momma for letting me be me!

So, in conclusion momma thank you for everything you have done,

Thank you momma,

For allowing me to

Be my momma's Son!

Original work Henry Harrison Epps Jr

IV

The usual suspect

I see you Mr police officer in my rear mirror,

Now what did I do today,

For you to stop me on my way?

Why is he stopping me on this road today?

I roll down my window as the officer walk up,

And I make sure I keep my way up,

So he can see that I am no threat

To him or me,

He says with a little malice in his voice,

Where you from boy, and where are you going,

I say I am from Army base,

And with malice in his face,

He looks me up and down with that ole
Southern frown. And
He says, you look like the usual suspect
Of someone who road a nearby store

And I say why you say that sir,
With dread in my heart, and
And he says all y'all boys look a like
You dark black man,

As he looks at my license I wonder will I ever
See my family again,
Because this man was not going to be my friend,
He calls in my tags and I sit and wonder

We live in two worlds, theirs and ours

With two different standards,

And two different laws,

Even at the malls,

The officer returns and say,

Here's your license now you be on your way,

Because you boys all look alike,

The usual suspects that I don't like!

By Henry H. Epps Jr

V

Love letters to God

Love letters to God,

How wonderful you are,

You are and always have been

The love of my life,

Thank you Father,

Love letters to God!

Love letters to God,

Oh how great thou are,

Like a long lost sweetheart my heart

Pant for,

Love letters to God

Love letters to God,

Thank you for my life, my

Children and my wife,

Love letters to God

Love letters to God,

Thank you for watching over me,

When I did not know, I needed watching

Thank you,

Love letters to god

Love letters to god, thank you heavenly Father for my

Mother and my father because they did the best they could

So I thank you father for the time

With my parents, Love Letters to God

Love letters to god,

Thank you for Chimere, Chanise, Charise, and Chatise

Kim, David and Eric. Thank you father

For my grandchildren, and

Foster children, thank you

Love letters to God

Love letters to God,

In all my getting Father, give me wisdom, and then a understanding, so that I may better serve you

Love letters to God

VI

A Father's day poem from my daughter to me

Ms. Chatise H. Epps

"A fire, a light
That does not flicker nor stir,
Has been ignited for purpose,
Centered in a place of four,

A prince, an heir
Instilled with a grace,
From his diminishing founder,
To generate a spawn for replace,

The prince obtains a consoling ardour,
Takes it out to perform his mission,
And new eyes behold the world,
Life smiles, new heirs has risen

The King seats himself in a mighty throne,

Light fills his eyes, fills his mind

That earns the attention of his new apprentices

And that of his attained"

Written by Ms. Chatise Epps

VII

A letter to my Father

Hey Dad, did I tell you I love you?

You were my hero and I wanted to be

Strong like you, thank you dad for being

My Father,

Letter to my Father

Hey Dad, dad I know you did,

Your best for me, and I thank

You father for loving me your son,

Letter to my Father

Hey Dad, thank you for trying to teach

Me some wisdom, and teaching me the

Golden rule, “to do unto others as I want others to do unto me,

Letter for my Father

Hey dad, I know you have finally found

The peace you were searching for,

And no more pain no more sorrow,

Letter to my father

VIII

Oh faith

Oh faith, faith where does thou be?

Oh faith, oh faith help inspire me,

Teach me to trust in the power of the living God,

Give me that faith that only comes from above,

Oh faith, oh faith helps me to see,

Help me to see the things I cannot see,

Help me the man God wants me to be,

Oh faith, of faith please helps me.

Oh faith, oh faith helps me to grow,

Give me to wisdom to sow the seeds that I must sow,

Teach me those things of love so I may know,

That your will be done everywhere I go!

Oh faith, oh faith fills me up, fill me up,

Fill me daily until I can take no more,

Fill me oh faith, fill me oh faith,

From the top to the floor, fill me oh faith

Until I can take no more!

IX

The Golden Age to come

The Golden age to is coming and time

Is changing like the leaves on a tree,

Times are changing for all people,

All people like you and for me,

The golden age is coming and it is coming very soon,

A time of faith, love and hope and brotherly

Love for all,

Time is changing its changing fast you see,

It's changing for you and for me!

The golden age is coming and it is coming

Very soon, it is coming for the world, just like

The sun at noon,

There is nothing to fear but fear itself,

The golden age of God of love, joy and peace,

An enlighten time will manifest

For all work to cease.

All the tears will be wiped away, and children can go out to play, a wonderful time is coming

And it is truly on its way!

X

This poem is dedicated to Chimere, Chanise, Charise, and Chatise

My little princess

My little princess oh how strong you are,

So sweet, so strong, little princess for all to see,

I believe in you and the power that you are,

To me all four of you are already superstars!

My little princess take the world by storm, create new

Works, write new songs, be great and be strong,

Never take no for an answer, do the work that is within you,

And never look back,

Because that is the princess in each of you

My little princess the sun is shining, wake up
Wake up, for the dawn is coming,
Be strong and work hard, and take the world
By force, be great and mighty,
My little princess!

My little princess can't you see, that God is watching
Over you, and smiling down on the women
That are to be, go and seek the world
For what you may glean,
So that one day you will wake up to be a Queen!

www.ingramcontent.com/pod-product-compliance
Ingram Content Group UK Ltd.
Pitfield, Milton Keynes, MK11 3LW, UK
UKHW020229250726
13967UKWH00001B/261